Flexibility
& Agility

An Integrated Life of Fitness

Core Workouts

Cross-Training

Eating Right & Additional Supplements for Fitness

Endurance & Cardio Training

Exercise for Physical & Mental Health

Flexibility & Agility

Sports & Fitness

Step Aerobics & Aerobic Dance

Weightlifting & Strength Building

Yoga & Pilates

An Integrated
Life of Fitness

Flexibility
& Agility

SARA JAMES

Mason Crest

Mason Crest
450 Parkway Drive, Suite D
Broomall, PA 19008
www.masoncrest.com

Printed and bound in the United States of America.

First printing
9 8 7 6 5 4 3 2 1

Series ISBN: 978-1-4222-3156-2
Hardcover ISBN: 978-1-4222-3162-3
Paperback ISBN: 978-1-4222-3200-2
ebook ISBN: 978-1-4222-8700-2

Cataloging-in-Publication Data on file with the Library of Congress.

CONTENTS

KEY ICONS TO LOOK FOR:

Text-Dependent Questions: These questions send the reader back to the text for more careful attention to the evidence presented there.

Words to Understand: These words with their easy-to-understand definitions will increase the reader's understanding of the text, while building vocabulary skills.

Series Glossary of Key Terms: This back-of-the book glossary contains terminology used throughout this series. Words found here increase the reader's ability to read and comprehend higher-level books and articles in this field.

Research Projects: Readers are pointed toward areas of further inquiry connected to each chapter. Suggestions are provided for projects that encourage deeper research and analysis.

Sidebars: This boxed material within the main text allows readers to build knowledge, gain insights, explore possibilities, and broaden their perspectives by weaving together additional information to provide realistic and holistic perspectives.

INTRODUCTION

Choosing fitness as a priority in your life is one of the smartest decisions you can make! This series of books will give you the tools you need to understand how your decisions about eating, sleeping, and physical activity can affect your health now and in the future.

And speaking of the future: YOU are the future of our world. We who are older are depending on you to build something wonderful— and we, as lifelong advocates of good nutrition and physical activity, want the best for you throughout your whole life.

Our hope in these books is to support and guide you to instill healthy behaviors beginning today. You are in a unique position to adopt healthy habits that will guide you toward better health right now and avoid health-related problems as an adult.

You have the power of choice today. We recognize that it's a very busy world filled with overwhelming choices that sometimes get in the way of you making wise decisions when choosing food or in being active. But no previous training or skills are needed to put this material into practice right away.

We want you to have fun and build your confidence as you read these books. Your self-esteem will increase. LEARN, EXPLORE, and DIS-COVER, using the books as your very own personal guide. A tremendous amount of research over the past thirty years has proven that the quality of your health and life will depend on the decisions you make today that affect your body, mind, and inner self.

You are an individual, liking different foods, doing different things, having different interests, and growing up in different families. But you are not alone as you face these vital decisions in your life. Those of us in the fitness professions are working hard to get healthier foods into your schools; to make sure you have an opportunity to be physically active on a regular basis; to ensure that walking and biking are encouraged in your communities; and to build communities where healthy, affordable foods can be purchased close to home. We're doing all we can to support you. We've got your back!

Moving step by step to healthier eating habits and increasing physical activity requires change. Change happens in small steps, so be patient with yourself. Change takes time. But get started *now*.

Lead an "action-packed" life! Your whole body will thank you by becoming stronger and healthier. You can look and do your best. You'll feel good. You'll have more energy. You'll reap the benefits of smart lifestyle choices for a healthier future so you can achieve what's important to you.

Choose to become the best you can be!

—*Diana H. Hart, President*
National Association for Health and Fitness

Words to Understand

endurance: The ability to keep doing something for a long time.

coordination: The ability to use different parts of your body together smoothly and efficiently.

stamina: Similar to endurance, the ability to put forth physical or mental effort for a long time.

Chapter One

WHAT ARE FLEXIBILITY AND AGILITY?

When most people think about fitness, they think of strength or **endurance**. They think of someone who can run ten miles as being fit. Getting in shape, they assume, means lifting weights or jogging. And all that's true. However, fitness has a different meaning too—flexibility and agility.

Flexibility is the ability to move your muscles and joints as far as possible. Of course, everyone has physical limits to their range of

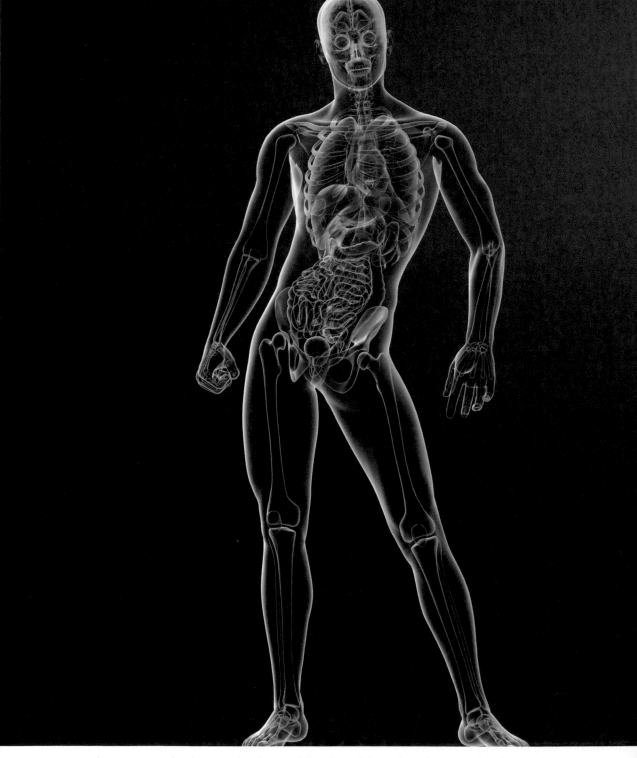

Without joints, the human body wouldn't be able to bend; it would always be in a straight-up-and-down position, like a board. Flexibility has to do with how much and how far each joint can bend.

10   Flexibility & Agility

motion, and there are movements most human beings can't make. But people can increase their range of motion pretty drastically with flexibility training.

Agility is a related but slightly different idea. Agility is the ability to change your body's position quickly and easily. People who are agile are able to run in zigzags or react quickly to a ball coming toward them. Agility is more than just moving fast, though. Agile people are also able to move accurately and respond to what's going on around them with skill.

Lots of other skills are involved in agility. **Coordination**, balance, speed, strength, and *stamina* are all important parts of agility. Without one or more of those skills, agility suffers.

Everyone can be more flexible and agile in some way. Some people are naturally a little more flexible or agile than others, but everyone can improve. Training for flexibility or agility will help you improve those skills.

With flexibility, every joint and muscle group operates independently of the others. And each joint has a range of movements, some of which might be more flexible than others. Even someone who can do a sideways split might not be able to do a front split. That person would need to work on her hip flexibility front to back, even though her flexibility in the other direction is impressive. Other people might have more flexible upper bodies than lower bodies, or vice versa.

OVERALL FITNESS

Flexibility and agility are two parts to overall physical fitness. If you are physically fit, you find it easy to move around doing ordinary activities, and don't find more intense movements too difficult in general. Walking to school isn't challenging physically, nor is climbing the stairs or biking around town. Physically fit people are "in shape."

Of course, there are lots of different components to physical fitness. The President's Council on Physical Fitness and Sports offers a definition of physical fitness that involves more factors than just the ability to healthfully and safely get through everyday activities. For

People who participate in marathons have to do some serious training first.

Flexibility & Agility

the Council, physical fitness includes flexibility and agility, bone integrity (strength), body composition (fat versus muscle), health of the heart, muscle strength, balance, coordination, and more. Most people struggle in at least one form of fitness as defined by the Council, which doesn't necessarily mean that they're not physically fit.

Fitness is something that can be improved, and it varies depending on a person's health. Someone who has been injured and has to lie in bed for a few months is probably not very fit anymore, even if he was fit before the injury. He can become physically fit again by exercising after he recovers. Going to the gym, running or hiking outside, or taking an exercise class are all ways to improve fitness over time. Any sort of physical activity repeated over time can contribute to fitness.

Some people take physical fitness even farther. Not only do they find everyday activities easy, they also can do extreme forms of exercise. They run marathons or half marathons, they swim for miles, or they play extreme sports. While these people are fit, they have gone beyond the levels of physical fitness necessary for normal life activities.

Fitness isn't necessarily all physical, either. Mental and emotional fitness are also central keys to living a healthy life overall. Healthy thinking patterns and behaviors are an important part of living a good life. Not being emotionally and mentally healthy may end up affecting physical fitness too, and vice versa. An active person who ends up getting in a serious skiing accident and injures himself might end up feeling depressed because he can't be active for a while. On the other hand, a person who has an unhealthy relationship with food and tries to lose too much weight will end up losing strength and weakening her body.

STRETCHING MUSCLES

Increasing flexibility actually just means stretching out your muscles in a gentle and safe way. As you stretch your muscles over time, they'll be able to work with your joints to move your body in a wider range of motion.

Flexibility exercises actually lengthen muscles. Of course, if you tried to lengthen them all at once and push your muscles past what they're

Muscle tissue

Skeletal muscle

Smooth muscle

Cardiac muscle

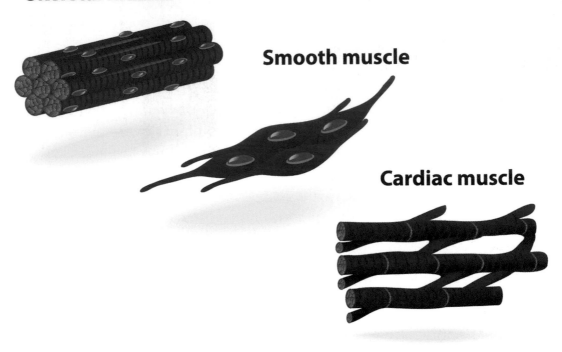

You have three different kinds of muscle in your body. Cardiac muscle is found in your heart, and smooth muscles are in your body organs. You can't control the movements of these muscles; they work by themselves, without any direction from you. The third type of muscle, skeletal muscle, is the one you have some control over. These are the muscles attached to your bones; they're what make you move every time you run, sit up, or bend a finger. Stretching these muscles will improve your flexibility.

used to, you could injure yourself and tear the muscle. Instead, flexibility training lengthens muscles a little at a time. After several weeks or months, muscles have gradually become longer to make you more flexible.

Stretching muscles comes in two forms—static and dynamic. Static

Make Connections:
Stretching and Growth Spurts

 Young people who are growing a lot all at once can benefit a lot from stretching and improving flexibility. During growth spurts, bones, muscles, and joints all get more mature. Flexibility training keeps muscle and joints lose, which can prevent pain and improve posture.

stretches require you to hold a certain position for a few seconds or minutes. They target specific muscles and can be fairly intense. You would be working one muscle group at a time with static stretching, so if you want to increase overall flexibility, you would need to combine several static stretches.

Professionals recommend doing a static stretch for at least twenty seconds. Then rest for about twenty seconds before doing the same stretch again. Muscles generally stay tensed for a few seconds before relaxing and feeling more comfortable in the stretch. Getting a muscle to relax over and over again leads to more flexibility.

Dynamic stretching involves more movement, like arm circles or jogging in place and bringing your knees up to your chest. Dynamic stretching warms your body up and stretches muscles gently. This kind of stretching is good for warming up before other forms of exercise or sports. It works larger portions of the body than static stretching.

MAKE EVERY DAY EASIER WITH EXERCISE

Flexibility and agility are great goals to have for many different reasons. We all use flexibility every day, all the time. You have to be

Can you touch your toes, either in a standing position or when you're sitting down, as shown here? If you can, than the muscles in your back and hips have good flexibility.

16   Flexibility & Agility

flexible when you bend over to pick up something. You need flexibility when you change your clothes. You're practicing flexibility when you sit down and stand up again. All these everyday activities would become a lot harder if you suddenly became more inflexible. Imagine picking something up off the floor if your hip joints wouldn't let you bend much, or your knees wouldn't bend!

These days, many people do a lot of sitting all day. We sit in school, at office desks, or in front of the computer or TV. All that sitting translates into a lack of flexibility. Muscles get tighter and shorter if they don't get their full range of motion regularly.

So, you might not notice how inflexible you are until you need to do something besides sit or stand. As soon as you have to touch your toes, though, you may notice it's harder than you thought!

Agility is also part of everyday activities. If you're late for class, you may have to walk quickly through the halls, dodging other students right and left. Or you're riding your bike and all of a sudden a car pulls out in front of you. Or you're in the kitchen and your cat darts out in front of you as you're walking with a plate of food. All those situations involve quick thinking and also fast body movements.

PREVENT INJURIES

Agility is key to preventing injuries, particularly during sports. If you have a split second to decide what to do as another person is hurtling toward you on the field, you can sidestep the impact if you're more agile. In the examples above, being agile might prevent you from knocking into another student in the hall, getting into a car accident, or tripping over your cat.

Flexibility, on the other hand, keeps your muscles loose and prevents injuries. Tight muscles can only move so far. If you ever have to move a tight muscle out of its normal range of motion, you could injure it. Maybe you're showing off for friends and you try to do a split or a move on a skateboard. You stretch your muscles farther than they're used to going, so you pull a muscle or a tendon or ligament, and then

This man has built up his muscles and has a lot of strength—but he may not have much flexibility.

you're embarrassed and injured. Proper flexibility training will keep your muscles from getting so tight and keep you ready for anything.

Flexibility and agility are especially helpful for reducing sports injuries. Athletes are always in danger of getting hurt, but a more agile and flexible athlete may end up getting hurt less often or less seriously.

IMPROVE SPORTS PERFORMANCE

People who play sports need a lot of fitness skills. Flexibility and agility are two that are often overlooked. Often, athletes just focus on strength training. They lift weights and do pushups and crunches. Strength is a part of overall fitness, but it isn't the entirety of fitness. The best athletes train themselves to be flexible and agile, rather than just strong.

Some sports obviously need more flexibility and agility than others. Gymnastics is a great example; gymnasts are very flexible and very agile. Even beginning gymnasts will need to work on those skills in order to do splits, backbends, and twists. Diving and figure skating are two other sports that require flexibility and agility.

Agility in particular is an important part of many sports. Some experts believe that agility is the number-one defining factor of a great athlete. A football player carrying the ball has to quickly dodge other players. Soccer, basketball, and hockey players have to weave in and out between players trying to guard their goals. In racket sports, players need to get to where the ball is going very quickly. In fact, playing racket sports like tennis, badminton, or racquetball is a great way to do agility training.

IMPROVES POSTURE

Posture is the position of the body when sitting or standing at rest. Posture can be good or bad—and most of us have bad posture! Bad

Gymnastics is a sport that requires incredible flexibility.

Flexibility & Agility

Text-Dependent Questions

1. What are flexibility and agility? Why are they important?
2. What are some of the other factors in overall fitness, besides flexibility and agility?
3. Name and describe the difference between the two kinds of stretching.
4. Why might you not be as flexible as you could be?
5. Which sports use flexibility and agility the most?

posture involves slouching or sitting hunched over, while good posture means sitting or standing up straight. Bad posture can cause difficulty breathing, back pain, and joint pain.

Exercise and fitness can help improve posture, particularly flexibility. A lot of the time, poor posture is caused in part by tightness in muscles. A flexible back holds upper body weight better and leads to better posture. Flexible shoulders and neck will also help you hold up your head and keep your back straight.

Good posture has a lot of benefits. You'll prevent back injuries and general pain. Fixing posture when you're young prevents a lot of pain when you're older. Good posture also projects confidence and self-esteem. A person who is hunched over doesn't seem very confident. But a person who is standing up straight and keeping her chin up is ready to face the world!

Chapter Two
EXERCISES TO BUILD FLEXIBILITY AND AGILITY

Flexibility and agility can improve overall quality of life—and luckily, you don't have to just give in and accept the amount of flexibility and agility you have now. You can take action and become more flexible and agile with a little training and dedication.

STRETCHING

If you're focused on stretching in addition to other exercise you do, make sure you stretch after every workout. Your muscles are warmed

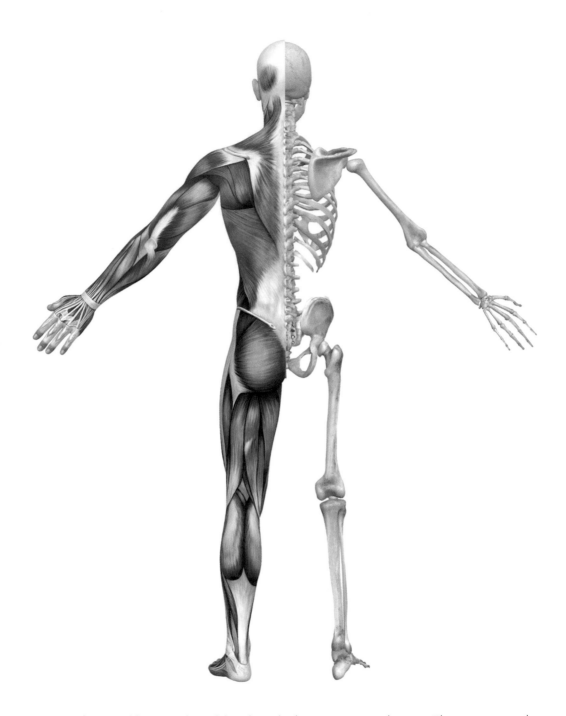

Your muscles are like stretchy rubber bands that move your bones. The more stretchy those "rubber bands" are, the more flexible you will be.

Flexibility & Agility

up and looser than they normally are, so after exercise is a great time to stretch. Stretch for at least five to ten minutes after exercising for the most benefits. Leave time after your exercise to get the stretches in, or otherwise you might cut them short as you run off to your next activity.

Stretching after a workout or playing a sport also helps you develop muscle and avoid being sore from all that exercise. After someone does exercise, especially strength training like lifting weights, her muscles are a little shorter than usual and full of lactic acid, which is created during exercise. Lactic acid is what makes muscles sore the next day after working out. Stretching lengthens out muscles so they don't stay short. It also gets rid of some of the lactic acid buildup, so the soreness won't be as bad.

Here are a few good stretches you can do. Combine a few of them into a workout to target different muscles.

- Forward lunge. Kneel down on one leg while putting the other leg at a right angle. It's almost like you're taking a huge step forward. Keep your back straight. Hold this pose for five to ten seconds, then stand up. Repeat on that side and then switch to the other side and repeat.
- Toe-touch. Stand straight with your feet touching. Bend at the waist and touch your toes (or get as close as you can). Hold for five to ten seconds and repeat a few times. For a more intense version, stand with your legs crossed and feet close together, and touch your toes.
- Quad stretch. Stand up straight. Bend your knee and bring your foot up behind you. Catch your foot with the same-side hand and hold it for a few seconds. Repeat and then switch sides.
- Seat stretch. Sit with your legs stretched out in front of you and close together. Flex your feet so the toes are pointing straight up. Stretch your arms out as far as you can and try and grab your toes. Bring your chin toward the knees. Hold for a few seconds and repeat.
- Twists. Sit down on the floor with your legs straight out in front of you. Bend your right knee and put it on the other side of your left

These people are doing twists, stretching out the muscles in their hips, stomachs, and thighs.

26 Flexibility & Agility

knee, keeping that foot flat on the floor. Place your left elbow on the inside of your right knee and twist to the left. Place your right hand on the floor behind you to help with the twist. Only twist until you feel the stretch, not until it hurts. Hold for as long as you can, then switch sides.

- Behind the neck. Stand up straight with a solid base. Bend one elbow behind your head so that your hand is touching your back. Use your other hand to hold that elbow and stretch it across your body. Hold for at least thirty seconds, then switch sides.

YOGA AND PILATES

Yoga and Pilates are two physical fitness systems that are great for flexibility. Different forms offer different flexibility benefits.

Many people practice yoga as a way to work out, but yoga is a lot more than just exercise. Yoga unites the body and mind through concentration and physical movement. It was first practiced in ancient India, and it is connected to Buddhism. Today, people around the world use yoga as a spiritual practice, as a way to calm the mind and fight stress, and as physical exercise.

Yoga comes in several different forms, and each offers some flexibility training. Some are slower and more meditative, like yin yoga or restorative yoga. In yin yoga, practitioners hold poses for five minutes or more. These styles are great for static stretching, and can target certain muscles that are tight. Other styles are more active and involve a lot of movement, such as vinyasa—or flow—yoga. The more active styles are dynamic stretching workouts, and take you through a lot of movements. It's best to combine different kinds of yoga to get the full flexibility benefits. Plus, yoga is great for strength training and core workouts. If you practice long enough, you'll be able to support your weight in handstands, through training and concentration.

Pilates is another physical fitness system that improves flexibility. Joseph Pilates invented it to help people build stronger core muscles. It also improves flexibility, along with endurance and balance. Since the early twentieth century, millions of people around the world have

This advanced yoga move requires both flexibility and strength!

28   Flexibility & Agility

Make Connections: Some Not So Good Choices

Not all types of exercise are good for flexibility and agility training. Biking and running are not the best choices for these goals, since both keep your muscles in shortened positions. When you're riding a bike, you never straighten your knees or move your hips or arms. Running is similar, although short bursts of running can be incorporated into agility training. These types of exercise can still be great activities for building other kinds of fitness, but if flexibility and agility are your goal, combine running and biking with other forms of exercise.

discovered Pilates and now use it as a way to work out. People like the variation in movement Pilates offers, and the challenge!

Pilates and yoga are often very similar. In fact, Joseph Pilates was inspired by yoga. Each one has some different poses though, and Pilates tends to move faster than yoga. Try both and see which one appeals to you. You might end up doing them both!

You can take yoga or Pilates classes at gyms, private studios, or at community education centers. Your school gym class might also offer an introduction to one or both. You can find DVDs and online videos that teach yoga and Pilates, so you can practice at home too.

DANCING

Dancing is great for both flexibility and agility, whether it's ballet, salsa, or swing dancing. Dancing gets you moving in ways you don't normally move, in a safe and repetitive way. That equals improvements in range of motion and also in how fast you can change direction while moving.

There are lots of kinds of dance—including hip-hop—and pretty much all of them require both flexibility and agility.

Watch professional dancers some time, and you'll see how flexible and agile they are.

A dance class will probably also include some stretching exercises to warm you up or cool you down at the end. You won't be able to do a split while dancing right away, but maybe someday you'll work up to it!

Look into taking dance classes or find a video online. Dancing is a great overall exercise too, plus it's fun. If you haven't found any other ways to exercise that you really like, try dancing.

STEPS TO AGILITY

Good agility exercises include several skills and techniques at once. For example, exercises should train you in acceleration and deceleration—which means how quickly you can speed up and slow down. Deceleration is especially important for changing the direction of your body quickly.

Agility exercises will also train you in visual focus. The direction you're pointing your head and where you're looking has a lot to do with how agile you are. When you learn how to focus straight ahead and move your gaze quickly to where you want to move your body, you'll make a big step toward agility.

Agility exercises train you to keep a low center of gravity, which gives you more stability and control over your movement. Good posture and a strong core will keep you agile. You'll also learn how to move efficiently so that you don't waste energy. An agile person knows how to move quickly with a minimal amount of energy so that he can keep going for longer.

DRILLS AND OBSTACLE COURSES

Drills are a great way to work on agility. Agility drills often involve cones, which act as obstacles you need to run around. Try some of these drills using cones, and time yourself each time you try them:

- T-run. Set up some cones in the shape of a T. Make the T about twenty feet tall and fifteen feet wide. First, run forward up the T.

Exercises to Build Flexibility and Agility   31

You can turn ordinary, worn-out tires into a fun obstacle course that will help you build agility.

Flexibility & Agility

Make Connections: Practice Balance

Balance is one component of agility that you can practice on its own. Better balance will help you have more control over your body and move it more quickly. One move you can do is to stand up straight and lift one knee off the ground until your thigh is parallel to the floor and you're balancing on one foot. Hold that position for as long as you can without putting your foot down. Then switch legs. Yoga offers balancing practice too, some even more challenging than this.

When you get to the intersection, quickly shuffle sideways to the right. When you get to the end, shuffle back the left, through the intersection, and all the way to the end. Then shuffle back to the center and run backwards down the T. This exercise gets you to move in four different directions!

- Cone taps. Place one cone in front of you and stand straight. Lift one foot up and tap the top of the cone with it. When you put your foot back on the ground where it started, immediately bring your other knee up and tap the cone with your other foot. You'll probably need to start out slowly, so you don't knock the cone over, but work up the speed as you keep going. Try and keep going for thirty seconds at a time.

- Zigzag cones. Place several cones in a zigzag pattern somewhere you have enough room to run around them. Space them out about six feet apart. Run toward the first cone. As you get closer, get ready to immediately shift your weight and run toward the second one. Try to make the turn as tight as possible. Start by jogging and work your way up to sprinting.

Exercises to Build Flexibility and Agility

One of the things that yoga does is teach you to focus on your breathing. Learning how to breathe properly can also improve your flexibility and agility.

Flexibility & Agility

To improve agility in a fun way, you may want to set up your own obstacle course. Include tires you have to hop through, steps you have to climb up and down, and barriers you have to duck under. Now time yourself! See how fast you can get through the obstacle course the first time you try. As you practice, you'll notice yourself getting faster and faster. Part of that is because you're used to the course, so mix it up every couple days. Rearrange obstacles so that you have to rely on your agility to get through it.

BREATHING

Proper breathing is a big help in flexibility and agility training. You may have noticed that when you become anxious or scared, you breathe

If you decide to commit to flexibility and agility training, it's a good idea to have some definite goals in mind—and a plan as to how you'll achieve them.

Exercises to Build Flexibility and Agility   35

Research Project

This chapter lists a few flexibility and agility exercises that are good for improving those skills, but there are lots more. Research other exercises or fitness routines. You can watch some online exercise videos or find helpful articles that include pictures of each exercise. Come up with your own list of options for flexibility and agility training.

faster and more shallowly. You're tenser. In this state, muscles seize up a little. Stretching would be a lot harder to do in this case, in comparison with when you're relaxed. Breathing has a lot to do with that.

Your body will be more loose and less tense if you breathe deeply and calmly. Deep breathing brings oxygen to your muscles more effectively too, which helps with stretching and flexibility.

When you breathe deeply, the lower part of your torso expands first, followed by your chest. Count slowly to four or five while inhaling and five or six when exhaling.

If you're having trouble figuring out proper breathing, try meditation. Meditation is the practice of calming the mind, to achieve awareness without thought. Meditation is hard to achieve, but it can bring all sorts of benefits, such as stress reduction, acceptance, and spiritual awareness. In meditation, people are taught to concentrate on their breath in order to let thoughts go and calm the mind. The same is true in yoga and in Pilates. Using meditation to learn how to breathe is a good way to relax into breathing while exercising.

Eventually you can practice "breathing into" muscles. That simply means focusing on the muscles you're stretching and imagining your breath moving into those muscles. Your muscles will actually relax more quickly and more fully, increasing flexibility faster.

Text-Dependent Questions

1. When is the best time to stretch during a workout routine?
2. How does yoga help improve flexibility?
3. What sorts of exercises can you do to improve agility?
4. How does deep breathing improve exercise performance?
5. What are the guidelines for doing flexibility and agility exercises? How often should you work on flexibility and agility?

HOW LONG?

Once you've committed to flexibility and agility training, you have to decide how long and how often you're going to train. First, think about how long each exercise and each individual training session should be. Then consider how long you want to train for, in terms of weeks and months.

The American College of Sports Medicine (ACSM) offers some guidelines for flexibility training. Exercisers should hold each stretch they do for at least ten seconds, working up to thirty seconds over time. They should repeat each stretch three to four times. And they should do flexibility exercises at least two to three days a week to really get the most benefits. The ACSM also recommends doing agility exercises two to three times per week for twenty to thirty minutes.

When it comes to how long you're going to exercise, you may want to consider setting yourself goals rather than a strict timeline. You don't really know how your body is going to respond to new training exercises, so it's hard to predict how long it will take you to become more flexible or agile. Regardless, flexibility and agility are something you'll want your whole life, so you're better off making these sorts of exercises into a lifelong habit. It will pay off!

Words to Understand

improvise: To make do with whatever is at hand.

effective: Working well.

cardiovascular: Having to do with your heart and blood vessels.

dehydrated: Not having enough water in your body for it function properly.

Chapter Three

EQUIPMENT AND SAFETY FOR FLEXIBILITY AND AGILITY EXERCISES

Before you dive in to flexibility and agility training, you should consider a few more things to make your experience more enjoyable and more effective. You may want to look into equipment that will help you train. Most equipment for flexibility and agility exercise is pretty basic, and you can **improvise** if you don't want to buy anything.

In addition, you'll need to keep safety in mind when you're training, just like with other forms of exercise. Taking safety precautions will

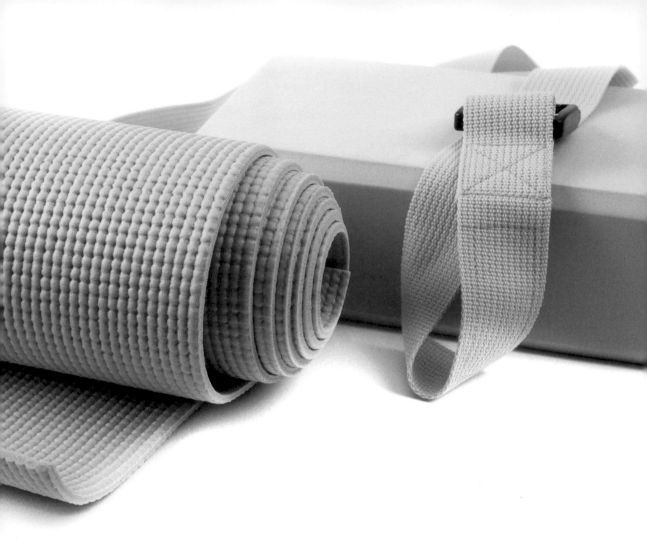

A mat, a strap, and a foam block are all the equipment you really need for yoga and Pilates.

ensure you can keep training over the long run, and you won't end up with any injuries that will get in the way of your progress.

THE RIGHT STUFF

Flexibility and agility training don't usually need a whole lot of extra equipment, so they are inexpensive ways to get fit. However, you may need a few things to take your workouts to the next level.

You'll probably need some good sneakers for agility training.

You may want some yoga or Pilates equipment. All you really need for these is a floor mat, which will protect you from the hard ground while you're doing poses. You could also buy foam blocks, a blanket, and a strap for support doing some yoga and Pilates poses.

For agility training, you may want to buy some cones or other objects to set up an obstacle course. You could also use objects around your house, though, if you don't want to buy any equipment.

Other equipment you should look into are proper clothes and shoes. Wearing the right clothes and shoes will make your workout better and safer. Wear comfortable clothes that don't get in the way of your movements. Different forms of exercise have different clothing guidelines. For yoga or Pilates, people usually wear close-fitting pants (yoga pants)

Equipment and Safety   41

A fitness trainer can help you make sure you're getting the most out of your exercise routine.

and a tank top or t-shirt. They don't wear any socks or shoes, so you won't have to buy fancy footwear.

For agility training that involves running, you'll want some good, supportive sneakers and loose clothing. Dress in layers if it's cold out, so that you can take some off once you get warm from your exercises. For dancing or other exercises, follow the guidelines of the class you're taking or the video you're following.

TALK TO PROFESSIONALS

Professionals can help you stay safe when it comes to flexibility and agility training. By talking to as many people as possible before you start, you can make your fitness routine safe and more *effective*.

First, consider talking to a doctor before starting any exercise plan. Your doctor will be able to tell you whether it's safe to start a fitness plan of any kind. If you have any health problems that could get in the way, she might give you some suggestion about how to make exercise safer. Or she might suggest you wait for a little while before starting. If you just broke your arm and you want to start training, she might tell you to hold off!

You may also want to talk about your weight with your doctor. The goals of flexibility and agility training aren't really to lose weight, so if your doctor suggests you lose (or gain) weight for health reasons, look for a different sort of exercise, like *cardiovascular* activities, which will burn more calories.

Another good professional to talk to is a trainer. Your doctor can give you advice on whether or not you should start exercising, and how intensely, but a trainer can give you more detail about the types of exercises you should do based on your individual needs and body. Trainers can be expensive, but using one will help you set and achieve fitness goals faster.

BARRIERS

Your body has barriers to becoming completely flexible and agile. After all, we can't just move any part of the body in any direction whenever we want. A good understanding of what it means to safely push your body and what your body's barriers are will go a long way toward making your workouts safe.

Some joints are just not meant to be flexible, or as flexible as you might like them to be. Joints are simply places where bones come to-gether, but some joints allow more movement than others. Your shoulder joints allow a lot of movement, but the joints where your spinal bones

Children tend to be naturally more flexible than older people. As we get older, we often lose flexibility—but with work, we can get some of it back.

come together only allow a little bit. You'll never be able to get your spine to be as flexible as your shoulder, no matter how hard you try.

Muscle length comes into play when determining how flexible you could be. Muscles do lengthen, but only so much. If you've gone through flexibility training and stretched out your muscles to the maximum, they're not going to stretch any more. Instead, you might start to lengthen connective tissue too much, and that could result in injury.

Your bones also determine how flexible you are. If your body runs into a bone while stretching a certain way, you're not going to get more flexible there no matter how much you try. For instance, everyone's hip

Make Connections:
When Are People More Flexible?

People's flexibility actually changes throughout the day. Most people are more flexible in the mid-afternoon rather than the morning or evening. Internal body temperatures rise a little throughout the day, and a warmer body means more flexibility. The same is true if you're exercising in a warm room versus a cold one. You'll be more flexible in a warmer environment.

bones are different sizes and tilted differently. If you try to try to do a stretch that involves some extreme hip movement, and you can't do it, your hip bones might be stopping you. It's good to know your limits, so you can move on to a different stretch.

Connective tissues are another barrier. When you improve flexibility, you're mostly working on stretching muscles. Your ligaments, which connect muscles to bones, and tendons, which connect bones, do not move as much as your muscles. They have a limit to how far they can stretch (which might not be very far at all), so that prevents you from becoming too flexible.

Age makes a big difference too. If you've ever seen a baby move around, they're a lot more flexible than adults—they can even touch their toes to their heads! Kids and young adults are still more flexible than older adults too. As we age, we get less flexible. One of the factors of declining health with age is due to loss of flexibility and increase in stiffness. Regular exercise can help prevent some of those effects, but some is just an inevitable part of getting older.

And people who start flexibility training when they're older will have to work harder than younger people to achieve the same degree of flexibility. That's a good reason to start training when you're young rather than waiting until you realize how much less flexible you are.

Finally, previous injuries restrict flexibility and agility. Any injury to muscles, joints, connective tissue, or bones can make a big difference in flexibility of a certain body part. To be safe, don't force a body part that has been injured to move past its comfort zone. You might end up reinjuring yourself. Talk to your doctor about the best way to exercise in case of previous injuries.

WORK UP TO IT

You might be tempted to just dive right in to flexibility training as soon as you get to the gym or stand up from your desk. However, you should warm up first. Your muscles aren't very relaxed yet, and you could injure them if you stretch them too much right away. You also want to avoid stretching too much too fast because you might injure your connective tissues. Tendons and ligaments aren't meant to be forced to stretch too much. Injury to these tissues will end up damaging joints and will make you less flexible in the long term. It's better to be slow and steady!

Instead, perform a warm-up for five or ten minutes. You could do a quick jog, or jump rope, or do some pushups or crunches. Your body will start to heat up, and your muscles will be more ready for stretching. Then start your stretching routine.

DRINK MORE WATER

Water is an important part of any exercise routine. Athletic performance is not as good when you're **dehydrated**, so drinking before and during any workout is a great idea.

You may not feel dehydrated or like you're slowing down, but studies have shown that even a small amount of dehydration causes a big decrease in athletic performance. The heart has to work harder when you're dehydrated, and injuries and fatigue are more likely to happen

Make Connections: Whole Grains

Grains are the seeds of certain kinds of plants. When a grain seed is harvested off the plant, it has three parts to it, called the endosperm, bran, and germ. Each part has lots of nutrients like protein and vitamin B. Then a lot of grain is sent to a factory, where two of those parts are taken out so that the grain can last a really long time on shelves without spoiling. All that's left is the endosperm, and all the other nutrients have been taken out. Whole grains have all three parts left, and are much healthier because they still have all the original nutrients.

when you're tired and slowing down. And you certainly won't be as agile as you can be if you're dehydrated!

Even if you're not feeling all that thirsty, drink lots of water while training. Flexibility training might not feel particularly exhausting, but your body is still using up energy and water. Keep drinking to stay hydrated and to keep your performance levels high. Start with a glass of water before working out, and keep a water bottle by your side during exercise.

Water is the best choice for hydration. Sports drinks have a lot of sugar, which isn't the healthiest choice. Soda is a poor choice. Stick with water during your workouts—it'll keep you hydrated without the extra sugar.

NUTRITION

Exercise is only half the equation when it comes to health—nutrition is the other half. Healthy eating is a big part of overall fitness and

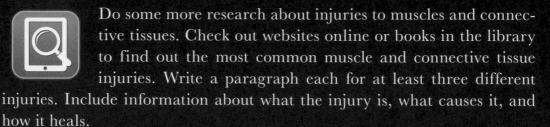

Do some more research about injuries to muscles and connective tissues. Check out websites online or books in the library to find out the most common muscle and connective tissue injuries. Write a paragraph each for at least three different injuries. Include information about what the injury is, what causes it, and how it heals.

exercise safety and effectiveness. You can train all you want, but if you have a poor diet, you're still not as healthy as you could be.

Proper nutrition has all sorts of benefits. Healthy foods and eating habits give you more energy overall—so instead of crashing at the end of every day, you'll have enough energy to do those workouts you've been meaning to do after school or on the weekends. You'll also have more energy to pay attention in class, to hang out with friends and family, and to get homework done.

Healthy eating promotes a healthy weight. Eating too much junk food leads to weight gain over time, which in turn leads to all sorts of health problems. Weight gain is tied to calorie consumption. Calories are measures of how much energy a food has. A food with more calories has more energy. People need about 2,000 calories every day to survive and maintain their weight. Any fewer calories and they start to lose weight. Any more, and they gain weight. Junk food has a lot of calories that fill us up without a lot of good stuff like vitamins and minerals. All those calories add up to weight gain. Exercise aids in keeping a healthy weight because it involves burning excess calories you eat—but you should also try to eat healthy to begin with.

Text-Dependent Questions

1. What sorts of equipment could be helpful to buy before starting flexibility and agility exercises?
2. Who are two good professionals to talk to before starting training?
3. How does age make a difference in how flexible someone is?
4. Why should you work up to more intense stretching rather than stretch a lot right away?
5. How is nutrition related to health and fitness?

Healthy eating isn't very complicated. There are just a few guidelines to remember, but no hard-and-fast rules you have to follow. First, eat as many fruits and vegetables as possible. Fruits and veggies are full of nutrients that keep you going and keep your body working right. Plus, they don't have unhealthy things like too much salt or fat, the way junk food does. Next, eat grains (especially whole grains) like brown rice, whole-wheat pasta, and whole-wheat bread. Add in some dairy if you can digest it, and protein sources, like meat, beans, and nuts.

Limit foods that have tons of sugar, salt, and fat. Soda, cookies, chips, candy, and movie popcorn are all junk foods. You don't have to stop eating food like that entirely, but limit them to special occasions.

Words to Understand

motivate: Encourage you to do something.
readjust: Adapt or change to account for something new.

Chapter Four

MAKING A PLAN TO STRENGTHEN FLEXIBILITY AND AGILITY

Y ou're more likely to be successful if you approach things with intention. If you want to get better grades, you'll have to make a plan to study more and finish all your homework on time. If you want to buy those new pair of shoes you saw at the mall, you make a plan to save your money until you have enough. The same is true of exercise and fitness. If you want to improve your flexibility or agility, you make a plan and stick with it.

If you want to be a good at martial arts, you'll need both flexibility and agility.

Flexibility & Agility

SETTING GOALS

Setting goals is a good way to be intentional about fitness. First, think about why you want to improve your flexibility or agility. What's the point of exercising in the first place? Try to be a little more specific than, "I want to be healthy." Do you want to feel stronger? Do you want to stop feeling achy after you sit in school for so long? Maybe you want to be a better athlete, and improve your performance in the sports you play. Working on flexibility and agility will help you do better in just about every sport. If you're a racket sport player, a football player, a soccer player, or a basketball player (among many others), you may specifically want to target agility. Gymnasts, ice skaters, martial artists, and others may want to work especially hard on flexibility.

Whatever your goal is, write it down somewhere you'll see it. Every time you see your goal, you'll remind yourself what you're trying to accomplish. Your goals will **_motivate_** you to keep going, even if you get frustrated or don't see improvement right away.

STAY MOTIVATED

Losing motivation is a huge reason people stop exercising. Making time to exercise can be hard, and if someone doesn't see immediate improvement or isn't having a good time, he might quit. Don't let that be you!

Setting goals and reminding yourself what they are is one way to stay motivated. You can also try other ways of motivating yourself so that you stick with your exercises. You could try working out with a friend who has similar goals. If you have a teammate who also wants to improve agility, practice agility training together. If your best friend wants to try yoga, go with her and try it out too. When someone else is relying on you to exercise with them, you'll be more likely to stick with your routine.

Make sure your workouts are fun. You might get bored running the same obstacle course over and over again. Change it up, or try a

It's easier to achieve pretty much anything in life if you start out with a good plan! It doesn't have to be complicated or fancy, but it should include the steps you'll take to reach your goals.

Flexibility & Agility

different agility exercise to keep from getting bored. If you're bored, you're more likely to stop working out.

You should also keep track of your progress. You might be two months into your fitness plan, and not see any difference in how flexible or agile you are. But if you write down your performance when you start, then you can really see just how big a difference two months has made. At the beginning, maybe you could only hold a lunge for ten seconds, but now you've worked up to twenty. Tracking progress lets you congratulate yourself and look forward to even more positive change.

THE PLAN

No matter how you're motivating yourself, create a fitness plan. A plan will guide your workouts and help you see the path to fitness. Your fitness plan doesn't have to be particularly formal, but you should follow a few guidelines.

In your plan, you'll need to turn a series of exercises into a workout or a training session. An exercise is one type of activity that has one particular goal and targets one part of the body or one motion. A pushup would be an exercise, or one yoga posture.

Exercises work most effectively if you put several individual exercises together. That way, you're working different parts of your body to improve your overall flexibility. Several exercises together in sequence make a workout or a training session. The training session has a larger goal than the individual exercises. For example, you might decide to do a toe-touching flexibility exercise in which you sit on the floor and reach for your feet. That one exercise would help your hips become more flexible and allow you eventually to touch your toes. Your larger goal might be to become more flexible overall, in all parts of your body. You would need to combine toe-touching with other flexibility exercises so that you could improve your whole body's flexibility.

A plan should also include a schedule. How long do you want to exercise for each day you work out? How many days a week do you want to work out? Actually schedule those days, so that they become

Create your own flexibility and agility fitness plan. You can look online for fitness plan generators or make one yourself. You may decide to ask advice from someone, like a coach, gym teacher, or fitness trainer. You should also search online for more specifics about putting together a fitness plan that sounds fun for you.

a habit. If you know you need to train every Sunday afternoon, you're less likely to forget.

Now combine your goals, schedule, and routine into an overall plan. You can write it down on your computer, stick a note on your fridge or desk, or even keep pictures of your plan around the house. The more

Make Connections: Online Fitness Plan Generators

A search online will come up with some websites that will help you create your own fitness plan. It won't be tailored to you as an individual, but you can usually fill out a form that creates a plan based on your experience, fitness level, gender, age, and more. Click around to find a generator that makes sense for you. Alternatively, visit with a personal trainer who can get you started on your own fitness plan.

Text-Dependent Questions

1. Why is it a good idea to set goals before you start a workout routine?
2. Name two goals you might pick for your workouts.
3. What impact can working out with a friend have on a fitness plan?
4. What is the difference between an exercise and a workout?
5. What should a fitness plan include? Why should you include each part?

time you put into planning, the more prepared you'll be—up to a point. Just don't plan so much that you never actually start exercising!

Your plan should be a combination of goals, workout schedule, and routines. Refer back to your plan every week to see if you're on track. If you're not, and have skipped some workouts or made them easier, that's okay. Just **readjust** and get back into your plan. Pretty soon, you'll be a more flexible and agile you!

FIND OUT MORE

In Books

Kajander, Rebecca. *Be Fit, Be Strong, Be You.* Minneapolis, MN: Free Spirit Publishing, 2010.

Kern, Betty. *Physical Education Nutrition and Activity Journal.* Uniontown, OH: Holy Macro! Books, 2007.

Mason, Paul. *Improving Flexibility.* New York: PowerKids Press, 2011.

Purperhart, Helen. *Yoga Exercises for Teens.* Alameda, CA: Hunter House, 2009.

Wechsler, Kimberly. *303 Tween-Approved Exercises and Active Games.* Alameda, CA: Hunter House, 2013.

Online

Exercise and Fitness for Young Adults
www.pamf.org/youngadults/health/exercise

OrthoInfo: Flexibility Exercises for Young Athletes
orthoinfo.aaos.org/topic.cfm?topic=A00038

Sample Flexibility Plan for Beginners
www.move.va.gov/download/NewHandouts/PhysicalActivity/P33_SampleFlexibilityProgramForBeginners.pdf

TeensHealth: Food and Fitness
kidshealth.org/teen/food_fitness

Workoutz.com: Speed and Agility Exercises
www.workoutz.com/category/speed_and_agility_exercises

SERIES GLOSSARY OF KEY TERMS

abs: Short for abdominals. The muscles in the middle of your body, located over your stomach and intestines.

aerobic: A process by which energy is steadily released using oxygen. Aerobic exercise focuses on breathing and exercising for a long time.

anaerobic: When lots of energy is quickly released, without using oxygen. You can't do anaerobic exercises for a very long time.

balance: Your ability to stay steady and upright.

basal metabolic rate: How many calories your body burns naturally just by breathing and carrying out other body processes.

bodybuilding: Exercising specifically to get bigger, stronger muscles.

calories: The units of energy that your body uses. You get calories from food and you use them up when you exercise.

carbohydrates: The foods that your body gets most of its energy from. Common foods high in carbohydrates include sugars and grains.

cardiovascular system: Your heart and blood vessels.

circuit training: Rapidly switching from one exercise to another in a cycle. Circuit training helps build endurance in many different muscle groups.

circulatory system: The system of blood vessels in your body, which brings oxygen and nutrients to your cells and carries waste products away.

cool down: A gentle exercise that helps your body start to relax after a workout.

core: The muscles of your torso, including your abs and back muscles.

cross training: When an athlete trains for a sport she normally doesn't play, to exercise any muscle groups she might be weak in.

dehydration: When you don't have enough water in your body. When you exercise, you lose water by sweating, and it's important to replace it.

deltoids: The thick muscles covering your shoulder joint.

energy: The power your body needs to do things like move around and keep you alive.

endurance: The ability to keep going for a long time.

flexibility: How far you can bend, or how far your muscles can stretch.

glutes: Short for gluteals, the muscles in your buttocks.

hydration: Taking in more water to keep from getting dehydrated.

isometric: An exercise that you do without moving, by holding one position.

isotonic: An exercise you do by moving your muscles.

lactic acid: A chemical that builds up in your muscles after you exercise. It causes a burning feeling during anaerobic exercises.

lats: Short for latissimus dorsi, the large muscles along your back.

metabolism: How fast you digest food and burn energy.

muscle: The parts of your body that contract and expand to allow you to move.

nervous system: Made up of your brain, spinal cord, and nerves, which carry messages between your brain, spinal cord, and the rest of your body.

nutrition: The chemical parts of the food you eat that your body needs to survive and use energy.

obliques: The muscles to either side of your stomach, under your ribcage.

pecs: Short for pectorals, the muscles on your chest.

quads: Short for quadriceps, the large muscle on the front of your upper leg and thigh.

reps: How many times you repeat an anaerobic exercise in a row.

strength: The power of your muscles.

stretching: Pulling on your muscles to make them longer. Stretching before you exercise can keep you flexible and prevent injuries.

warm up: A light exercise you do before a workout to get your body ready for harder exercise.

weight training: Exercises that involve lifting heavy weights to increase your strength and endurance.

INDEX

ABOUT THE AUTHOR AND THE CONSULTANT

Sara James is a writer and blogger. She writes educational books for children on a variety of topics, including health, history, and current events.

Diane H. Hart, Nationally Certified Fitness Professional and Health Specialist, has designed and implemented fitness and wellness programs for more than twenty years. She is a master member of the International Association of Fitness Professionals, and a health specialist for Blue Shield of Northeastern New York, HealthNow, and Palladian Health. In 2010, Diane was elected president of the National Association for Health and Fitness (NAHF), a nonprofit organization that exists to improve the quality of life for individuals in the United States through the promotion of physical fitness, sports, and healthy lifestyles. NAHF accomplishes this work by fostering and supporting state governors and state councils and coalitions that promote and encourage regular physical activity. NAHF is also the national sponsor of Employee Health and Fitness Month, the largest global workplace health and fitness event each May. American College of Sports Medicine (ACSM) has been a strategic partner with NAHF since 2009.

PICTURE CREDITS